MR. DICK'S KITE

ARNOLD RATTENBURY

Shoestring Press

Typeset and Printed by Q3 Print Project Management Ltd, Loughborough, Leics
(01509) 213456

Published by Shoestring Press
19 Devonshire Avenue, Beeston, Nottingham, NG9 1BS
Telephone: (0115) 925 1827
www.shoestringpress.co.uk

First published 2005
© Copyright: Arnold Rattenbury
ISBN: 1 904886 13 2

Shoestring Press gratefully acknowledges financial assistance from Arts Council England

CONTENTS

Many poems in this collection are dedicated to or in memory of old friends, but the book as a whole is, once again, for my beloved Sim

Acknowledgements

Most of these poems have been written since 1996, versions of some appearing in periodicals and of others in the collections *For John Clare* (1997), *Poetry in English* (1999, Critical Survey's festschrift for John Lucas) and *The Way You Say the World, a celebration for Anne Stevenson* (2003). 'Mozart Pieces' is earlier than the rest: performed by Simon Callow and myself as part of the 1991 Mozart bicentenary celebrations, its intended publisher failed that year and the glut of mozartiana at the time advised that it be set aside. The twelve poems making up 'The Frigger Annexe' adopt 24-line forms I had used in *The Frigger Makers* (1994) but were written much later. In the same way two recent poems in Part III clearly descend from 'Mozart Pieces'. And there are more of these things. Neither Mozart nor Friggermakers, in forms each has appropriated, ever now let me alone for long.

I: LOOKING

'We were peeping at the circus,' muttered Louisa haughtily, without lifting up her eyes, 'and father caught us'.

'And Mrs. Gradgrind', said her husband in a lofty manner, 'I should as soon have expected to find my children reading poetry'.

(*Hard Times*)

GOOD WINTER

for Dinah

Winter is now the best time.
Year has happened,
whatever they say, whatever the claim
for Spring, this comes first and that second.

And what after all does anyone know
of the nature of Then,
the thing supposed to happen? How things go
is never exactly what was meant.

So now, when all is possible
is the best time.
Frost may possibly fail to kill
whatever it is we planted and like to assume.

Or there is always the chance
of change lain dormant
waiting some later Spring, happen years hence.
Time, and others, pick the moment.

OLD MAN AND DAUGHTER

The old man huffing as they walk
is eighty, his daughter fifty. They talk
of her son near twenty – almost equal
       these distances. Working

their way, gauche, from the Quai Voltaire,
questions of age take on an air
of histories that have passed here,
       there – o, anywhere

for they must pause a lot. It's hot.
Much has changed, much has not.
A little further, and Revolution
       put hundreds of monks to the chop.

*

Some of the buildings in that heat
lean back slightly, old habit sweating
down walls to where the pair of them's passed
       present along the street.

On upper floors long shutters, grey
and blistered, open beside stiff drapes
or close dark secrets up, so age
       has little or nothing to say.

Down at their level – Commerce: antiques
and fashion mainly, as you'd expect
if history stopped. Dim-lit boutiques
       play them at hide-and-seek.

*

Unequal distances now – of day
to day; one fad or belief to another;
visit to visit; Musée d'Orsay
       to St-Germain-des-Prés;

Impressionists to Picasso's head
for Apollinaire; dear Nancy, who loved
Apollinaire, to myself, he said
       to himself (his daughter heard).

*

Upright, buildings are able to keep
their secrets better, shuttering tight
on the privacies indoors – weep,
        laugh, wake, sleep.

But then there is this business of trees
rooted somewhere above ground level,
burly in walled gardens, at ease –
        above the shop! if you please

where nothing's supposed to be above
Commercial here, on this hot day,
the present. Pasts went hand in glove
        with difference, so Love

and Revolution happened as needs
must – though never were needs greater,
however we pity the monks, bleeds
        the heart, takes a seed.

                    *

Passing the Palais Abbatial
(one abbot a king) the past, house-tall
to the old man and his daughter, now
        seems wholly believable.

They smile agreement in each other's eye.
Time slides slowly down the sky.
Along the pavé as they pass
        their lengthening shadows lie

that then begin to climb, rap
at the blistering shutters, rat-a-tat-tat.
Not in our time? Her son's perhaps.
        Walk on, content with that.

Note: 318 priests were hacked to death at St-Germain-des-Prés in 1792. The
Musée d'Orsay has a huge collection of Impressionist paintings. The open-air
Apollinaire memorial at St-Germain-des-Prés is a Picasso sculpture. Nancy is
Nancy Cunard, rebel and poet. The king who had been an abbot and occupied the
Palais Abbatial was Charles V, known as the Bourbon.

ON THE CUT, OTHERTON

for the navigators Jack, William, Paul

Silken the black moves, its ripples
as we pass silk-shine,
and in them reflection silkily tipple-
distorts, loop for line.

Beneath surfaces, history lies
that built canals like this,
though no navvy encampment survives
except some cemeteries.

Past Otherton, 'Happy Beryl', 'Bert's
Folly', 'Promises' rock,
riding at anchor the swishing skirts
of passage. Carefree, slack,

the moorings map out a pleasure lake
where men once worked Litt-
leton Colliery, for its unsafety's sake
the well-known Slaughter Pit.

Willow springs vertical from fallen
boughs of willow, beech
stand by the water yet somehow fail
the willow and do not weep,

and birch beside the towpath screw
their barleysugar-stick
reflections, silk to the tongue, into
a black past rhetoric.

PROSPECTS

Hard to explain, he said, to one
who never knew the way things were.
See the top of the mountain there, *Craig Wen?*
A line of trees ran up to that from here –
once. Not all the way in fact
but seemed so, for gardening's intended vista
put in a sapling fringe, now hacked
right back, to mask the middle distance.

There on the other guarding edge,
much as it now stands, the long beech hedge,
clipped and rigid, though twice they let
a beech spring to make proper trees
above that regular line. The pair stands yet –
not brisk as they were, nor bright and breezy
versus propriety, their arms akimbo.
They too have been de-limbed.

Surely, I asked, there was good reason?
Ay, he shrugged. And always is,
hadn't you noticed? Never mind weather, season,
crop-plan, access, nor what the trees
themselves might offer: shelter, shade,
harbour for birds (much lacking here
until that long vista was made;
lacking again now, I fear).

He left me then, words hooking
on brambles rife in nature's chaos beyond
this curtilage. A way of looking
taken within his stride, gone
for good his prospects. Common enough,
this loss of a manufactured plan
pointing through nature to nature as, in rough
ways, poem or Good Old Cause can.

THE LADEN ROOF

People live there, so the house
has warmth. Snow begins to loose
itself at the ridge towards avalanche.

Along the eaves an overhang
grows heavy, ready to fall and crash
on innocent founding grounds below,
but the air freezes again.
                         Heat
has been insufficient. The moment's passed
and snow remains, weighing us down,
a government which all the fires
of belief have failed so far to shift.

WELSH HONEY BEES

Wasps, we said, enraging further
a buzz-mongering disturbance
made of the upstairs windowspace –
which means, in this most ancient place
to live, a three foot cube of light,
so thick the walls and wide
the windowsills. More like a public square
of protest, such was its battered air.
Or they mistook the proper buzz
of homecoming – to a nest? – above? –
in the roof?
           Shut the window.
Now they bombard the glass from outside into
here; but somehow infiltrate,
singly, under the eaves of slate,
down through old-fashioned ceiling-boards,
distracted, turning away towards
the light where riot fellows are crowding,
then skid on panes, trying for out,
wanting the air. Each morning I sweep
them, dead by the charnel-heap,
from the windowsill.
           Send
for someone from Pest Control in the end.
'Wasps?' snorts Merfyn. 'These' –
his voice is fond – 'are Welsh Honey Bees'.

*

Across from here the *frydd* lies languorous,
forestries fling dark shawls
shoulder to lap that once were all a-fuss
with farming, gashing that told
of quarries, caveways to gold-
mines, property work-aproned in proper walls.

*

9

There's much performance: hose, canister,
ladder from Merfyn's van. Panic
continues its angry buzz of despair
about his head in the out-of-doors air
above us. He purrs over his quivering
work in a running-softly river
of Welsh.
            'Terrible waste', he says, descending.
'Honeycomb's there, but a bend
beyond me. Had 'em before, you have',
he asserts. Memory pulls at its ravelling
fact with fiction. One summer
seems to remember itself, and then another
but nothing demonstrative as this.
'*Duw!*' says Merfyn. 'I've give 'em the kiss
o' death, for I can't reach the comb
and get 'em out. It is their home,
you know.
            'Saucy, them little queens,
have to be off with the lads as green as
maybe. Can't have two in a hive –
eat her alive, she would,
the old'un. So pass by here and catch a whiff –
or throb, is it? – and in … No, stiffs
won't worry 'em … Yes, lie idle
for years a comb can, waiting on new arrivals'.

                        *

            Farms have shrunk; brambles itch and scab
            the gashes; rowan and birch
            splint up the caves; and walling, whether slab
            or drystone, breaks its teeth
            on posts and wire. Beneath,
            beside, no work, no people, how you search.

                        *

10

A last few of these slim-bodied
natives beat the bounds of the open window,
nuzzling but puzzled. Quiet –
and who perks up to rumours of riot
now? – seems absolute, except
for odd solos by the odd birds left
this mountain.

        Merfyn's parting shot:
'Name you a beekeeper'd pay a lot
for such a comb: he'd come in winter,
lift off the slates, take it into
his *cadwraeth*, re-slate you, go –
if you was to let him. Don't want to know
how much, nor Pest Control'.

        That's it,
then? Sell them away in private? Kiss
off nature's, history's course, and the buzz
of whatever it is a people does
towards dignity? Under this ancient roof,
there where a mountain's working loose
of sense, here on a page
devoid of programme, we can rage
all right, but not pretend – no less
traitors than those that made such a mess
of mountains. No real belief, no ease
rests on this abeyance of bees.

INDOORS

Breaking up garden stalks for kindling,
papery skins pull back to curl
until each break becomes frill-ended –
as honeysuckles are, petals
head-tossing back, or the way flames whirl
and spit, bridling at difficult coal.

Fire catches. Smoke spires up enough
to indicate foxglove, delphinium,
tree-mallow, ghosts of themselves that cough
and flute, ancient asthmatics rough
about a collapsing pith, phlegm
in the throat, hiss, gargle. Pathos –

but the room warms. Things alight
on their own brightnesses, less and less
on memory than present delight:
my dark-haired girl this white-haired darling.
Images? Flowers? Nor is this poem
the one that I began to write.

LATE

i.m. Jonah Jones, sculptor

When only the black poplars have shed
their leaf, in late afternoon,
light comes, low-lying like a shepherding
dog through tall grass, to the lawn.

Against these late-in-the-year stretched
shadows each blade sits up clear
as an etch. The undersurfaces of beech
are bright-lit instead of their

better-known glossiness. Weatherboards,
guttering under the eaves, that high
long unbroken shelf, the sky:
all are lit from the treading levels –

as if the earth were being mown
by light, old knowledge stooked and ricked
in the old way, everything else unknown,
fresh-sculptured, an artefact.

Utopian? No – for that's imagined,
while this latter-time light that sweeps
an underclass of things is fact
undreamed of. Nothing to do with sleep

though the end of light growls and advances
on lawn, roofscape, beech-branches.

THE PLASTERERS' GANG

at Plas Mawr (1577–1581), Castell Gwydir (by 1580), Maenan (1582), the Vale of
Conwy (Royal Jubilee Year 2002) – chiefly from guidebooks

for Penny and Adam

Enter the tremendous Plas today, and wealth
smacks at your eye, good as be told –
by moulded plaster chiefly – Rich
    we are: why play stealthy?
Plasterers, thus encouraged, grow bold,
say Sure, old goat (one wife dead, so another hitched),
slap up bobbydazzler Bedrooms for each,
and Hall, Parlour, Great Chamber? Suit yourself.

Can't have been cheap, this large plastering gang
hauled up from England, nor need be.
The commissioning Wynns had conquered all
the Vale of Conwy, bells rang
    them from here to eternity
at lovely chapels of theirs up hill and mountain wall
to east, south, west. And then the call
of court, of London. Wales go hang.

               *

Skilful, these plasterers: made moulds, slapped on
big Tudur Roses, Lion, Stag's Head,
Three Eagles of Gwynedd, Bear and Staff,
    Beheaded Englishman –
all the devices a pair of marriages had bedded
here. And sonsy mermaids of Conwy
in seaweed bikini pants (caryatids, my eye:
workman's devising, sexy, a laugh).

Wages swam down Afon Conwy with fish,
field-crop, mine-crop, God-crop, other profits.
    Wynn-wealths came in by ship
as well, through the Menai Straits, coffered
with foreign pickings on royal missions.

14

Even the plasterers might have been shipped this way
along with plunder out of Cadiz
and plaster – by the hundred ton, they say.

But wealth gets absent-minded. A chimneypiece
hangs Tudur Roses down from the ceiling
as from a gallows; fleurs-de-lys
up-end themselves to droop exhausted cock
and balls; and the hot pleasures of blood released
      gouting from an English neck
by English plasterers are plain as pikestaffs.
No Wynn presence holds them in check.

Do other visitors guess more than garish
boasting, the boldness of mouldings puffing off
ambition, success, wealth – rarities
      wages were paid out for?
I only ask of Now (more often
of Then) because of ambivalence a-lurk
in skills. That over-carved coffin
in Conwy church: widower's grief or mason's work?

        *

Our gang moves: to the Wynn base, Castell Gwydir,
where little is left of plasterwork;
then to cousins at Maenan (named
for an abbey got of a dissolution got of a Tudur),
      and the moulds recur. The same
forms wrap and pillow walls and roof – cruck,
spur, purlin – like so many dissolute monks
in a clover of duvets choked on eider.

Other craftsmen of course worked all three sites:
masons shaping their chosen rock,
carpenters felling and sawing particular oaks,
quarrymen splitting and trimming slate
to roof these courtiers in. But the plasterers
differ. Incomers? Veins of subversion –
      is it? – among Welsh strata
also tip-trucking income at the wide Wynn purse.

Does wealth always contain its end in the end,
get wholly plastered, not merely drunk
        on power? So there is hope
in such a time of spectacular overspend
as ours – Capital's cargo sunk
in some Menai Straits of dream? Suppose
fatcats hanged from a ceiling; their own prose
choking ad-men; fuzz in a blue blood-royal funk.

                *

Fifteen seventy-seven to eighty-one, Plas Mawr;
Gwydir by eighty; Maenan in eighty-two.
And then the plasterers disappear.
None of their moulds, their curlicue
        arse-over-tips to be seen.
Time becomes night, and blacks them out. So
they are dead of old age perhaps or hanged for abuse
of kings – if subversion is what they mean.

Extend the dates. Stuarts decline
from Tudurs, but offer no chopped-off English
king until sixteen forty-nine,
wartimes ahead. But back from that triumphant finish
by fifty years, in sixteen hundred, here,
        suddenly, our gang again!
The same figures precisely, plastering rhyme
on reason – at a merchant's house – in Ipswich!

Looking back – to Plas Mawr, Gwydir, Maenan –
from where we are, I don't suppose
(but it is possible) those marvellous plasterers
shared either your desires or mine,
though good to think so while we gasp and admire.
        Coming home, thus late
in the day and history, things could develop faster
while shadows gather and we, too, wait.

FLOCK

Ewes bellow outside tonight
and the grey-wool lambs bawl back. I think
the ewes began it, sheared to the white
today, and shrunk to tiny-seeming
beside their young.
              In the black ink
of night, seek comfort or lie dreaming.

All sound has taken on the acoustic
of indoors, as might be mountains
for enclosing walls, night for a roof,
rain's soft furnishings.
              And the cause?
That bleated silenced protest? – amounting
only to Nature on all fours

with human nature. Shorn? Oh, ever.
Quiet descends through whiffle and cough
and wheeze toward sleep.
              Under the covers
darkness teases, knits up its wool.
If nothing comes of protest, then profit
conquered, and we are animal.

ACKNOWLEDGING PHOTOGRAPHS FROM FRANCE

for Terry Corbyn

Both prints I see: a sturdy housefront dressed
    over-all in foreign leaves;
then pleached limes raising fist upon hoorah fist
    like a home crowd's padded gloves.

But chiefly, by absence, see the photographer
    clear, no uniform,
fists ungloved for camera-clicking or a lover's
    holding close and warm

to him. Just so, the sky up here holds Wales
    its friend. Come any weather
mountains return the hug, even in gales
    fitting snug to each other.

Odd in a way. These parts of Wales are desert
    now, disquarried, under-
farmed, float no more ships, their young departed
    or hooligan, small wonder.

Beyond this window *Craig Wen* erects his nipple
    cairn, long flanks protect
the secret *cwm*, the coombe, the river let rip
    at a rapids, then calm 'til the next

rapids. Into this room, this viewpoint that isn't
    his, and cannot be,
the pictures yes but the bare hand too reaches
    this bareness, befriends me.

GARDENS

i.m. Sam Sherwood

Under a sun in sky a-scud
over Wales the day you died, trees
not long in leaf closed in on us,
cut off the waiting distant views
of winter – when trees grow skeletal
and you are there, ourselves here,
plain as houses.
                    Now, enclosed,
engreened, in leaf, in grief, that long
view runs back inside the head
for it has nowhere else to run –
back over lives. But then explodes
in colour, pops on a garden's poppy,
stops for that fruit-ripe gaudy laughter
of your perpetual ribaldry,
dazzling all the enclosures you knew,
and runs a-mock.
                    The fact, dear Sam,
is plain enough: things grow when planted –
flower, die off to skeletons,
then laugh again – provided merely
some gardening care. Those distant views,
as well as the near, continue. Here,
in places tended with belief
(and disbelief) by you (and us),
blossoms fruit, trees are in leaf.

From beds, tousled, leave-me-alone,
root and bulb and corm and seed
wake up, break out, upstand, flaunting
banners obstinate as the deep
old causes you and ourselves hold true –
us in both versions of a wake;
you, in only one, asleep.

19

GILBERT'S ARK

between visits to the garage-studio at Tyddyn Bychan of David Gilbert, sculptor
in wood, including brief notes on a few of his pieces, particularly smaller ones, and
mention of a recently added annexe

I

You get in by a small side door
known to sailors as the entry-port,
though there are signs towards the back
of almost garage-like door-tackle
for the drive on/drive off end of ferries.
Noah himself – or so the series
of models I've seen suggests – removed
most of a deck and forcibly shoved
his couples up wooden ramps or dropped
them in from the sky. Gilbert adopted,
I think, the ferry method once,
for one of his couplings is immense;
but now, not only for singles but for two
by two, the entry-port must do.

II

Layout inboard is crowded, gangways
meandering, cabins cribbed, and the hang
of things hard landlubber work
to achieve, especially in so much dark.
And then you stumble on *Mr and Mrs
William Blake* pretending this is
their garden, this wooden meantime cabin
(or so a label would have you imagine).
Someone eases the hatch-covers
offering strips of light about us;
more figures leap out of blocks of wood,

each block somebody's habitude.
Teak, laburnum, oak ... Why, the quayside
bollards, even, were lignum vitae!

III

You have to understand, of course,
that a block of wood is what the person
carving can make of it. Uncut,
each cabin is empty so far, or shut.
But carved, o my! Here one stands proudly;
others make love (sometimes lewdly);
there runs one in panic from door
to door through shafts of wood-light, poor
bugger; and many in tall shadowy
cabins climb Wittgensteinish ladders,
while others teeter on a spinning globe –
figures here for ambition, hope,
soul-searching, terror, love, shame,
balance. And no two the same.

IV

Long since, discussing matters between
each expedition for specimens
they lacked – perhaps a mate for this
or that aboard – at quayside, *Mr
and Mrs Noah* were godgift clear
about what would eventually appear
in their two by twos. But matters change.
Later species developed whole ranges
of yet more species until, fly as
they seemed, the Noahs now seem liars.
We're not inclined to think of the deluge
presently threatened, and surely huge,
as godsent, listable, or other than
the unaided feat of species Man.

V & VI

Storm approaches, craft creaks
at its moorings – hopefully one of those freaks
of weather more puff than threat. And yet
it's black above, that red's no sunset.
More like disaster bent on running
from door to door in panic, or shinning
up ladders.   Another dam has dropped
a river level to scorch its crop,
famine on parchment; another flood
from kill-forest making illegible mud
of whatever was written; or brother brother!
another greed, another another
war, so come on! wha'd'y'mean warning?

Just such a clear sail-away morning
as now, after storm, finds us afloat
on the flood. No hint of harbour in sight
in this weird interval: victualled,
hatches battened, bejewelled by the spittle
of voyage.   On deck, we who survive –
Mr and Mrs Gilbert, my wife
and I – unlike the Noahs, work on
for there's no end to the kinds of Man,
which is to say the cabins, breed:
newcomers climb impossible chimneys,
peer into depths, top pillars, twin
faces twin across deep gouge-outs between.

Small wonder the Ark has had to take
a shed-like dinghy into its wake.

VII

The rest is supposition. A bird
will arrive with news of landfall, we've heard;
then waters recede and tip us, for we'll
have hit high slopes and so must spill
some cargo – though all being wood will swim

that do not walk ashore, none jetsam.
And pray the future natives make
out what was intended, once they awake
to the job of settling: all this understanding,
fear, dependence, wonder
wrested from wood; from wisdoms, attempts
to hang on to common in uncommon sense.
Lose greed. Better the place to be.

(signed) *Mr and Mrs Rattenbury*

WILD

Speedwell spills a slick across
the heave and slap and sag of grass
where the daisies fleck. No protest occurs:
earthworms rise fishily, and birds
dive for their dinner.
                    We should be mowing
but the day is one for nothing-doing.

At a disorderly shore where the lawn
beaches itself, Sylvia's bright
dwarf hyacinths flirt and swank in the sun
while Amabel's campanulae bate
each other, cliff-scrambling the housewall,
the barnwall.
                    Who needs to be useful?

Fieldfound, Judy's cowslip steps
to the green-blue water's edge, toe-dips
then paddles, soon to swim off on the bosom
of the deep, that long-bourgeoisified ism
it was born to.
                    Left-alone grass,
grow on and swell, be buoyant for us.

BONFIRE

Choose your definition. 'A good
fire' or 'A fire of bones' – even
perhaps of sacred bones, making it good
in itself; or feed it the sad remains
of once-good fractured furniture.

The best are always set in gardens,
of woody un-compostible things.
Their scent is one that hangs in hedges
scarflets of chiffon, privacies,
the history of where they came from.

Both definitions, then, for the bones
of things are not to be forgotten
ever. A past always makes good –
not now? then later – and there are flowers
thriving on light deposits of ash.

BODLOESYGAD IN MIST: II

for Chris Pilling

Less a mist descending than earth
rising through pallors: this plume of breath,
meant to take to itself the colours
of speech, one white among others

and soundless now as a paper's blank.
Familiar faraway things – the bark
of dogs at *Bryn Melin*, *Bryn yr Odyn*'s car
starting – startle by seeming near

as these two feet on the ground. Birds,
wing-flat, hurtle and smudge and blur
the air in passing attacks, lost
for the song-and-dance of calendar custom.

Even midges, scribbling at eyes
are somehow erased, virtual, rough-white
just-cancelled pencillings, no nip.
Only feet move step by step

by custom. Habits of thought go upward;
similes, images once coloured
fade through the pallors, then bleach – as if
nothing existed for comparisons with.

*

A foot stumbles at an ill-placed wall
'til now considered immovable –
but why? Distance so close, birds
for instance so changed, what's permanence?

*

No doubt if one went further afield,
looked back, mist might appear to be fleece
brambled as happens to sheep, or wire-
barbed bandaging as happens in war.

except here is no other distance
than footstep. This changing of circumstance
to white-out even removes *Craig Wen*
from forming the near horizon.

There are no limits here. Walls
as well have got their comeuppance – until
some weather-change, some blowing in the wind,
an end to footloose, surrender of mind.

Then mist drains darkly into the soil
that bore us up, leaving a spill
of dew – on spiderweb, grass, petal –
flashing with neonate lights, come-get-us.

Small evidence, but much repeated
at dawn, rain-break, sunlight through sleet,
and it is real and so can cope
with the charges: Utopianism and Hope.

SMALL CHANGE

Dog-roses are back: in hedges
or through and over drystone walls
that soften or harden the edges of all
roadside properties hereabouts,
they scatter themselves, showers of small-change,
gleeful, on-looking child-eyes.
                              Change
indeed, for this is the year after all
when no blackbird sang, no heron
lit on the field between here and the river,
black grouse no longer called that cross
between barndance and parliament where heath
had conquered farming.
                      So much has been loss
to the filth of greed, rattle this fact
in your pocket: dog-roses are back.

II: LISTENING

'… As to the amount of strain upon the intellect now, was you thinking at all of poetry?' Mr. Wegg replied, musing.

'Would it come dearer?' Mr. Boffin asked.

'It would come dearer', Mr. Wegg returned. 'For when a person comes to grind off poetry night after night, it is but right he should expect to be paid for its weakening effect on the mind'.

(Our Mutual Friend)

WINDOW

Wales climbs steeply behind the house
so that my room at the back
frames field, tree and barn – no sky. Dawn
is only slivered pink on white bark.

Above the field, a road passes
unseen, and a motorbike pinks unseen
scaring the birds that take their breakfast
on the sill here, or stop to preen

on the barn roof. "Heck-heck"
goes a blackbird among them. "Pink-pink"
says my birdbook – quite wrongly, I reckon:
the sentence continues "by way of warning"

although the blackbird returns heckling
each morning. I am idle, you think,
to lie here, play with words – well, one word.
I am unwell in fact, not in the pink

but am not idle either. Yes, meanings
tumble like a bunting with a crust
or politicians with what a colleague said.
Last night the sun set Wales red.

INSIDE CHAPELS, LOOKING OUT

for Harry Chambers

Sills to windows happened high
from the ground. Only when standing for hymns
might even a proper adult see
how the world went, how the bee hums,
how aquilegias nod to the weight
and work of bees – outdoor things, bright
and beautiful at knee-height.
                                        Had
but the pews let jumps rise higher, dear god
what a thing!
                          But all the rest was good:
the scent and crinkle of much-leafed books;
histories of bottom-polish so the wood
shone holy; music, split-up, hung-
over words.
                          Had there but been in those looks
the outside chance, the oddsong.

MOZART PIECES

for Simon Callow

Backnotes to this sequence appear at the end of it

Considering K 175 child's play

Power's puppy, parasite,
I am arrested by what I do
caught in flagrante delicto –
so nearly fragrant, so nearly delight.

> Piss ? What a rainbow soars
> to "would" from "all that I can" !
> Mere boy, so nearly man.
> Fart ? What a trumpet blares !
> Of God's creation ? Doubt
> it, whatever they choose to spout

who have earth's power. Their promises
are for the Kingdoms Come of prayer,
not physical as my body's are
or music's Paradise here is.

K 216: the proper location of heaven

Handy, randy, riddledy – Whoa!
How can "the Adagio

have fallen straight from heaven" ? I'm
earthy and like it. If I rhyme

childishly in adulthood
where men grow soulful, why a fellow should

(if he can) work toward synthesis.
The Adagio fell out of this

body I live in – couple with,
for heaven's sake. (That heaven's no myth).

33

Hallibo, crackabon, discum, dan
Why so belittle man ?

To enlarge God ? We, wo, wac
Little archbishop, give me the sack.

Callow's aria for 'Amadeus'

The wig, the hop, the giggle, this acting stuff
got up by sniffing a text, is well enough

but o Thalia, o Melpomene, where
in this all-farting shitshanking partial view
of the great man (and of myself too)
does the music come from ? Whatever I think or dare
say, partial is partially true.

And now I fall. In love. On Shakespeare's sonnets.
By which I mean am beautified: upon its

own this love makes unridiculous me.
Gotcha, you little bugger ! The flimsy envelope
author and I had made bursts open
with love or ... call it music. Fragility –
say wig, hop, giggle – wraps any human scope.

K 271, written for a lady called Jeunehomme

If there's to be a harvest, seed goes in
to a soil well ploughed, much furrowed to begin.
Then all the world, young man, is ours to win.

There are the two great acts and interval –
the sowing time, the golden time, and the full
summer between, trembling, a crucible

34

cupping its drop of peace as the furrow cups
a seed. But tiny Bewick ants deplete
the implanted grains of truth and cart belief

away, or wind licks cold on peace.
Then seed comes up and the world is a fleece of gold
like everything foretold for Abraham –

or not. We only know when the harvest's in
that all young men strut out on the earth to win.

The Adagio, K 285

A breath's plume, secrets a boy sings,
this flute, while the strings go widdershins
to scuff a path in the plucked stubble:

> as Bach gave harpsichords his double
> violins to twang; as God
> in the setting of bitch bickering earth
> to lovely Son; as drips in snow;
> as fat men hold intact their bubble
> dreams like any us, though shod
> on bananaskins; as pence to worth;
> as children chatter whose eyes glow –

her prickling nest rests the round dove
of peace. Coarse cursing accompanies love.
Good and government could go hand in glove.

K 279b and lost or stolen originals

Once were no fences. Lamplight forms a pool,
now, for the old commonsense to fill.

There it was innocence that people lost
when, with daylight, the fencers came. It wasn't

Elysium but was entire, be-dozened
by Calendar Customs, and no counting the cost

cash being nothing. Yes it is gone. But what
you remember, or hear of, or hear, or guess, is not.

"Tatterdemalions upon a Common"
the vicar said, wishing to write them off;
but that is unachievable, even by theft,
so long as any is left whose will can summon

under this lamp the lost or stolen song
that never finally goes in the long long run.

The Soloists' Dialogue, K 364

O weep for Paradise
with me, that distant place
that's war – if this be peace.

Sky sleeps in the river-face,
rivers buzz or are still
and honeyed as bees, and grace-

notes gather in a trill
or fall in a waterfall
of scales from off the sill

of eyes. Truncheons are tall
green trees in Paradise.

O brother, speak no more
of that far place. That's peace
and pain while this is war.

1779: Gilbert White, Bewick, K 365

Near Mayday, Gilbert White observed
a Black-Winged Stilt, stuffed it with peppers,
weighed it, was puzzled; and Bewick carved
two inches square at least ten acres

and a flea in the foreground. Also about
this time Mozart, having the same
insatiable habits of marvelling
and an almost identical touch, came out
with his double piano concerto. Fame
is odd, you know. It was the same Spring.

And yet – neither Bewick nor Gilbert White
has much to say about despair.
Though they persisted, everything is delight.
For Mozart, the agony is always there.

K 387, the first repayment of debt to Haydn

Still I must imitate to learn
and only later come to own

a debt to old original.
By then of course what truth's to tell
will be something about myself,

no longer copywork or theft.
Meanwhile – while I'm mean, I mean,
absorbing him, trying to melt
him back to ore – sometimes, between

the bars, design will seem a minting
almost his, however quint-
essentially mine. He'll take the hint

perhaps, and come in turn to own
a debt, pay me in my coin ?

On his modulating upwards

How did he get up there ? Sun
filters tremblingly through the leaves
distracting vision, but not the fun
of trying to discover what the vision is.
And when you reach him there, he's gone.
Where is he now ?
                        You feel – you half-
feel – ancient, until comes skittering down
an 'O how sad to be old' on a laugh
tumbling like sunlight.
                        Go where the sound
came from ? The air's turned peaceable.

All this time you are learning the tree
itself, a thing rooted in ground
that seemed not, but is, all natural.
And the lad swoops down to prove it. Whee!

K 413, K 414, K 415

I am my own man now
that lately stooped to others,
kept and milked like a cow

or cash. Maygamers, brothers,
workers for provender,

I'm yours, the ones I love as
Customs in Calendars
are loved; the world made over
in play. My talents are
for plough, or put-to-clover,
or goods you sweated for

at a lathe. Halloo ! Hallo,
those rude commonwealths over
that lately stooped so !

K 426, raised by a friend under A.O.B.

The Brother sends apologies
(being dead), and a short note
on a matter he believed would arise
from the Minutes.
                    Liking a pun, he wrote
"Brothers, I have been looking Bach
and blow me, the bugger was looking forward.
So it's a stiff shit in the dark
to think the Present anything more
than a stopgap. ..."
                    Note ends. Beckoned
by furies of work no doubt, young stinker.
Never say Die would he, nor deny
Art its revolt. For sure he'd second
Brother Brecht's motion: "You think a
thing Utopian ? Ask why."

The Andantino, K 449

All the world over there must be some longing
between lovers beyond the immediate we,
each lust uncover more than you and me.

The mind stretches, wonders may never cease.
To live is hunger and imports its own ease
in a world lacking the pact conditions of peace.

And if an appetite import some pain
to peace, why Man's sweet reason will come again.
It is the parched of Art cry out for rain

to God. The reasoning man uncovers here
huge definitions extending how what is dear
is dear, and his embrace. Religion is fear

and what is fact is fact. The point of despair
is the point at which he starts to go from there.

Allegro ma non troppo, K 449

Quickly. Thirst and a gnawing hunger
for love dawdle a way to death.
Behave always as if younger
than that, incapable of running out of breath.

But under the quickness, less quick.
If never slow as the love-sick
still slow enough for thought, pride,
belief – as might be in the fellow at your side

as quick as you, as little dead
as you, as prone to go a-giggle in the bed ...

but always thoughtful be. Older
far perceived a perfect fit
for heaven round earth, then over-bold –
pray mercy – made sad balls of it.

K 456, written for a blind girl called Paradis

Let you be Paradise to the fingertips
and let your heart not grieve where it cannot see,
be blind and turn all the world over to me.

> Toss a penny, and the heads or tails
> offer their touch of luck to you.
> Eyesight tucks up the night with nails
> of gold but spins into starless blue
> like a bird, like a tumbler to Parson White
> despite his decorous bib. Or an inch
> of seasoned wood, summerset aright,
> is whole counties for Bewick to clinch.

Preserve you as you are, see that you make
this versy world, keep closed your eyes from wake
and weep, so as your heart may never break.

The Storaces' lodgings, K 464

Clear now that France was racing
to regicide, England afraid
of industrial revolution, and facing
Mozart a shift from court to trade
for sponsorship.
                Catastrophe looms
but passes as unremarkable here
in the Storaces' rented Vienna rooms.

Dittersdorf calls, young Attwood, dear
old Haydn. Nancy and O'Kelly rehearse.
Stephen tackles a violin riff
from Mozart's ink-wet staves.
                                    Reverse
perceptions, then. Join in – as if
their laughter were yours, man in the street,
and a king's poison your meat.

The Andante, K 482

There is a drought in us
cracking the human clay
that only the blessed cussed

rain can mend – that drowns
sometimes, or is too late
sometimes, or sometimes frowns

in cloud like pities that dare
not weep, or try but fail
to weep, or weep elsewhere.

But there are seeds in us.
Stuck in the human clay
is life – impervious

but life – for there is pain
and this idea of rain.

Maydays 1786 and after, K 492

Whatever else a dry world may say
the show opened, and on the first of May,

and was subversive. We had to cut the plot
to suit an emperor's ban, but managed to keep

the harlequinading in and, under a sweep
of music, disrespect and some pop.

Nine performances only. Pisspoor payday.
Life goes on. You try to forget. Then "Mayday

Mayday" becomes the cry of all distress
at sea. I'm dead by now, but not one whit
astonished, protest no more the heart of it –
although, how forget togetherness ?

We'll go no more a-roving, non piu andrai,
Figaro, Figaro, you, anyone, I.

Parson Woodforde introduced to K 492 later

By dark, Parson Woodforde returns from Norwich,
shit-scared of footpads, dreaming of food (of course),
also confused by the voice of Nancy Storace.
Her concert lingers in him.
                              Good Green Goose
well stuffed with Larks, two Turbot, a Dish of Quinces.
Starts at a shadow. Gives no programme alas
though tunes run in his head.
                              So we must guess.
Given the state of country audiences,
safe to assume perhaps some Kiri Te Kanawa
hits ? But surely one Susanna aria.

Mozart wrote for that voice, in italian, in german,
that english lark to soar above all birds –
Figaro stuffed with sopranos frangling the words –
above all food, all footpads – and the Sunday sermon.

K 503, beginning Allegro Maestoso

By custom it is the gods that do the making;
and now that God with all his pups does not,
then I must make. Join back the waters to the aching
lands of summer, and where the seed is hot

and damned, near-cracked with thirst, build my cathedrals
octaves cool where culture put the rows,
and paint west windows kaleidoscopes for those
that can't, or won't, or kneel too low, to heed
sweet reason raining from the texts I preach. I'll sing
them hymns to make the masonry of clouds ring.

Or tear my cathedrals down again, unfrock
all dogmas, laugh in the streets to see dogs go
a-begging in their collars to the good godsbodies, men.
Word and world turn over. Such powers I know.

Summer 1988, K 543

All summer the crops have filled
and fields turned gold and been harvested.
Famine and drought have been a yield
elsewhere, though.
                    What can be done for the dead,
this Abyssinian done-for, but pity's
weeping movement – conscience – between
those outer movements – bolder, if brittle
sometimes ?
                    Well-fed is obscene.

Hearts lift to a music that would
make good if it could. But here and there
what more is to do that gild a kiss
for comfort ?
                   Multitudes are required for good.
There's little more to dare
alone, in symphony or sonnet, after this.

The bicentenaries of K 550, K 551

Only the intention matters
when living stops and that was that

stick, stock, stone, dead.

It's the inanimate that live
afterwards, scribbled things once given

hand, heart, spirit, head.

At any time all knowledge is
the sum of the arts and the sciences

updug, invented, thieved, inbred

and no time later can subtract,
even through ignorance, the enactment

black, white, thinblood, red

of the works of Man – whatever the air
we breathe or hear, anywhere.

K 595 played in the Himmelpfortgasse, 1791

In March he came to play at the Gate
of Heaven, in a nick of time (by
the account of most biographers) –
though for the young, nine months to wait
in a nick's too long for a trial set in the sky
and the only key St. Peter's.

The piece he came to play was new.
No saints. This is for Here and Now

as Then was. All the keys there are
for opening anything are here. He can play fool
in the many mansions, weep or
giggle, be grave, be gay. Yet so far,
though he has broken every gatekeeper's rule,
he is unsung outside by low people.

Forty dances, one hymn, KK 559–611, 618

You want to dance, masters ? Dance.
The ballroom shuts at five in the morning.
After an overloaded night
or life, you want to pray ? Or chance
my praying for you ? Light has been dawning
on me, too – so that's all right:
here is an *Ave verum corpus*
quick as a flash harry.
                    But o,
for those among us that well know
how days after have no more purpose
than the lives before, change is essential:
conspiracy by Lodge, if need be,
should Time find time and I the speed
of magic for anything so immense.

Magic on the Common, K 620

Keep close to the earth as possible,
avoiding fashion, ear to the groundling's tune.
Touch scenes with a slapstick to turn them turtle.
Fingers crossed, dress up in blackface. Soon,
soon the magic will come.
                              For me, a flute
brings it, but barricades might do so, or any
Transformation Scene or prop.
                              These things
are for a common place, the harvest's fruit
being gathered in – a Musichall or Penny
Theatre – day, night, levelling.

Always protest, for life must where a man
lacks dignity. Do so always with joy,
for that is the point of protest. And if you can,
seem innocent as if still a boy.

Quam olim Abrahae promisisti, K 626

If all the world, all you, all me,
all justice, all estate, all wealth –
excepting dreams – is all there be:

if life's a religion to pursue
towards God, if there is God, then you,
God, must honour, as I do

all mine, all your great promises,
and give your penitent Abraham
and all this penitent seed of his

47

life out of life at last, and the birth
of a golden Paradise on earth.

And this demand alone – most sweet,
most jolly – gravely paupered to church
do I repeat, repeat, repeat.

Köchel's Adoration

Bewicky things like snails
or dragonflies or less
weigh up my botanist's business;

and Gilbert White's frail scales
my mineralogies –
that need no silver trails
or wings to glint like philosophies;

and splinter-patterns of rime
piano as cat's-paw water,
shake-notes, arpeggios like laughter:

minute things that combine
to reveal me nature's nature;
and human nature, mine
by gift of a tiny god, a creature.

Backnotes

I use Köchel numbers throughout partly because 'K 482' is pithier than 'Concerto for piano and orchestra, No. 22 in E flat major', partly to simplify looking things up if needs must. The following notes may help meanwhile.

Mozart lived 1756–1791; Bewick, wood-engraver 1753–1828; White, naturalist 1720–1793; Parson Woodforde 1740–1803. The coincidences here have got in among several poems.

The vicar in K 279b is the Rev Samuel Wesley, another contemporary; the phrase is quoted from a letter to his more famous brother John and disparages a popular low-class culture of the kind *The Magic Flute* celebrates. Scattered references to calendar customs, blackface, counting games, maygames, groundlings and so on are also to assert alternative low cultures of the time.

Anne and Stephen Storace were Mozart's great friends in Vienna. Anne, possibly his lover, was the original Susanna, a part he wrote for her. Returning to England she toured widely, and Woodforde heard her at Norwich.

Three references are *not* contemporary. The phrase about the Adagio K 216 is from Einstein, *Mozart: his character, his work*; and Brecht's "motion" in my K 426 – properly "If anyone thinks this is Utopian, ask him why" – is from *The Messingkauf Dialogues*. Both narrative and slang in 'Callow's aria' are lifted from his own moving account of *Amadeus*, Shakespeare's Sonnets and Love in *Being an Actor*.

Some poems play on information in their titles. Thus – KK 271 and 456 were written for the ladies named; K 279b is a suppositional reconstruction of lost or stolen work; *The Marriage of Figaro* did open on a Mayday; Mozart introduced K 595 in Himmelpfortgasse, a name meaning Gate of Heaven Street, on March 4 and died, almost exactly nine months later, on December 5, 1791.

A THING IN BACH

There is a thing Bach does – after
some chuntering, baskets creaking with veg,
puffcheeks, rattle of keys, barter –
far, thin, on the very edge
of sound, a long note swelling
'til it fills all the dry air in the market,
a tune makes itself up as it spills.

No benison rain, no God's jacket
round a plump opinion (though Bach of course
was all in all religious: "Alas
winter so mild", he wrote, "few calls
upon me for any requiem mass").*

Others do the thing too, but this
winter is Bach's, who summersaults the whole
world over to my irreligious bliss

proving that revolution is practical.

Note: to George Erdmann, Leipzig, 28 October 1730

THE FAR SOUND

for Sheila and Tony

Just for a moment, between the front
door and the shed, that sense of country
rustling all Gwynedd countrysides have,
something unseen that's less than movement.
Outside, that day, rain had run
into almost-silence, hinting again –
at what?
             Indoors, we'd spoken of other,
more certain things than possible weather-
change; of pointlessness, of the gaps
we live in, loss of purpose, lip-
service to old causes, dead
movements. Chilled, I'd gone to the shed
to fetch more logs, and then, mid-stride:
what was it lay hidden in the outside's
quiet?
         Ah but of course! the river
below our neighbouring fields, alive
with storm-emptied clouds, headlong, careering
away to other conditions than here,
uprooting much tangled matter, upending
rocklike committees.
                        I should have mentioned
this when I returned with the logs –
for your home too half-hears that rushing
distant optimism unblock
time for a moment, in a moment's hush.

III: READING

'What do you think of that for a kite? ... I made it. We'll go and fly it, you and I', said Mr. Dick. 'Do you see this?'

He showed me that it was covered with manuscript, very closely and laboriously written ...

'There's plenty of string', said Mr. Dick, 'and when it flies high, it takes the facts a long way. That's my manner of diffusing 'em. I don't know where they may come down, it's according to circumstances, and the wind, and so forth; but I take my chance on that'.

(David Copperfield)

AT PWLLYMARCH

for Anne and Peter

First came 'Leaving Pwllymarch', listing the details
               of littleness belonging;
soon after, 'Carol of the Birds', some nine of them
          being specified, but others singing
               in a quiet way to be so.
Everything small, missable, quite unconcerned with fame.

And a small place both poems came from: heart of a vast,
               high up, where few go
save birds and lesser unnoticed things (and sheep of course
          for this is Wales); the poor-to-do
               but history-touched, past-
present in a present never as big as the past was.

Later, coming indoors from a cold day in a cussed
               time, places were laid –
cutlery, glass, crocks, winebottle, servers for veg,
          carvers – in patterns history made
               custom to all of us,
each place verse-like, end-lines rhyming at the table-edge.

High up as this, the ice-cold sun let clouds pass
               outside; details froze
on the marsh for sheep to mumble into their slow motion
          behind our backs. And then sun chose
               exact pinpoints on glass,
metal and crock to spark the table with constellations –

my poem of listings this, not yours – Cassiopiaea,
               Great Bear, Little, Orion …
reduced by the details of place, poetry, Here, Out There
          to manageable size for try-on
               images of Hope,
Legend, Belief (if any is left anywhere).

You'll ask – you did of an earlier version of this – what
               had we spoken of to reach
such huge conclusions? As to the talk alone, not much;
          but the small coupled buildings beached
               in a vast historic plot
of mountains and time, poem on poem present-touched.

1791, GAP, 1793

Later, when music had died on the air –
in this case, two years after they chucked
its body into a lime-pit – Clare
was born, another set up to be fucked
by the system. Yet even enclosed in the bin
at Northampton, he went on musicking.

Closure's not final. Earlier
the church had enclosed: escape from her
turned some Masonic. Now, for Clare,
when they enclosed both earth and the air
he breathed, the birds that flew in it, trees
on nickname terms, he turned to reason,

its heritage, old musics, metre, rhyme,
tempo. No madness, nor a lime-pit this time.

PRAYER

Marlowe, Marlow, Marloe, Marlo,
take me on as dumped cargo,
throw me at least a middling line;
Marlen, Marlin, and spikiness; Marlyne,
and abusive powers, so that the bastards cringe
under a lash of tongues; Marlinge,
should ever I cry off sick
when ineffective; Merlin, for magic;
scrooge me Present and Past, ghost-holy Marley,
though not into charity, Marlie, Morley,
that has no Future save pi-jawly —
until at the last: amen, Morle,
that I may sometimes be any good at all.

Note: The 13 Marlowe spellings are as listed by Boas (1940). More (and a longer prayer) must have been discovered since.

A NOTE FOR ANNE STEVENSON

"….. an I (and, of course, equally an 'eye')",
    you wrote of Elizabeth Bishop,
And a him (equally a 'hymn'), you'ld have to write
    if ever your pen
should walk its way up the steps of my
    pulpit – except you never knew father's mish-mash
of person, vision, 'No Bishops', or delight
    in sermons, music, pun.

SIXTY STONES

on leaving St. Tanwg's church, Llandanwg, Ardudwy

Fifth century their names, those Irish christians,
Llandanwg their best of anchorages.
Travelling east they left us gravestones,
claimstones, namestones, milestones – no images.

Ingenuus, Equester, the names most readable
here on a shore now hidden deep
in sand-dunes and marram and wrack and beach-pebble
edging this later flawed grey rink of sea.

More stones – sixty are known – stood or were laid
through centuries, from here to Chester,
while all the roman habits died
save name-forms for lichen-spread, salt-blister.

By bronze-age, celtic and roman roads they took
off into imperial collapse –
to judge by the rareness of some stone's rock,
important people, up to princes perhaps.

But commonsense it seems to us, this leaving
marks in a lately deserted space
pointing towards a goal you believe in:
not Chester for us, but a Regain'd Paradise,

Gonzalo's version of Prospero's Isle, Marvell's
Bermudas, the greek for Nonsuch, Clare's
Helpston (at least the Commonwealth),
Gurney's trenchmate longings, Morris's Nowhere.

Again, but reasonable to by-pass the massif.
Their stones were left at Tomen y mur,
Ffestiniog, Cerrigydrudion, as if
Ingenuus, Equester had passed by or died there.

Still the mountains remain, and the weather's mist,
which parts now to boast of later
scars: quarries and cemeteries
not single stones but sixties on sixties, slates

filled up with chiselled evidence, black slabs
of status and progeny that prove
hard spellings often enough, rubbing
old eyes through bramble at cloud-heavens above.

All that gone too. Quarries no longer breathe
and bleed with men. Profit has gone
elsewhere to satisfy its greed.
Village streets march away like retreating romans.

At the top of *Cwm Cynfal*, echoing voices commend
themselves, bounce off a spoilheap on wealth's
mountain – Now is like any Then –
to poverty's mountain. Capital's balanced itself.

And into this void came we, more centuried
on the job than Ingenuus, Equester:
seventeenth, eighteenth, nineteenth, twentieth,
now twentyfirst. Majoritised – so we are

with names deep-carved into language richer and rarer
than any rock. If only two
be allowed me to balance that Irish pair,
let them be the commoners Ivor Gurney, John Clare –

though Shakespeare, Milton, Marvell, Shelley, Blake
also marked mountainous routes towards …
Egalitaria (to make
a name up)? Ardudwy is a-nudge with words.

There's Shelley at *Tan yr allt*, fighting reaction
from Mab's lines. And the wooden bridges
that Clare's railway carpenter son
joined us across the rivers Mawddach and Dwyryd.

There's Morgan Llwyd in his cruck-built *Cynfal Fawr*
with poems for Colonel Jones. his friend
the regicide – for that was the year
not one but all kingdoms of the earth would end.

Ingenuus, Equester ..... Blake. People who plan
new worlds as whole as this, know
what we have to know, learn what we can.

How much further from Llandanwg must the cold sea go?

DOG WITH A BONE

after reading Peter Constantine on early Chekhov

Gorki, according to Bert (who met him often),
used to say to tiro authors plaguing him,
'Improve yourselves by trimming the works of Tolstoy'.

Now it appears he got this notion from Chekhov
who did precisely that; and Gorki loved
Chekhov – more, was it, than he worshipped Tolstoy?

Once indeed, in the garden at Sochi, he watched
as Chekhov tilted his upturned hat to net
for sunbeams filtering down through the trees; and Gorki,

fearful of causing him to spill his catch,
tiptoed away. Odd to imagine one
as austere as Tolstoy beside that Chekhov, that Gorki.

Bert, you should know, was A.L. Lloyd, collector
of folksong, to whom finding a text to cherish,
not smithereen, was the issue. According to Bert

Gorki himself got *War and Peace* corrected
to something like *Vicar of Wakefield* length – not
that it mattered. (As I did, you would have loved Bert

and worshipped the other three). Time's necessities
change, he'ld say, so imitation's a crime –
in folksinger, fatherfigure, tiro, even Chekhov –

innovation the virtue. Discoveries
like Bert's, or love's, are there to sniff and dig
and gnaw for the marrow – in Gorki, Tolstoy, Chekhov.

THE ROYAL SOCIETY, 1770

The Honourable Daines Barrington, one of a clique,
an FRS, presents the Society his view
(poking about in the matter as might do
Gilbert White in a corpse) of the boywonder freak,
Mozart.
      And only a little later, especially
for the infant prodigies Charles and Samuel Wesley,
arranges a concert showing them off alive.

To think him entirely obsessed with beautiful boys
would be unfair. Nothing suggests he enjoys
anything – even those letters that began to arrive
last year from the Reverend Gilbert White himself,
who's fifty.
      These he encourages, this well-born
dilettante. They form – look on the shelf –
Part Two of 'The Natural History of Selborne'.

MEANTIME

"... In the meantime, you'll be so good as to lend me your bike for I find we're
running late for the revolution"

(Jamie O'Neill)

All new incident seems high and white
on such a day: mountain ash
and hawthorn blossoms, looping spikes
where kiftsgate will strap the oak, splashes
about high nests.
        On blue there stand
white clouds no bigger than a man's hand.

Lower down, significance
in colour is muddling. Canterbury
bells, cornflowers, monkshood dance
on the air – for a boy, for the Virgin, a tory,
the megrims.
        Often a spring day's weather
stops putting two and two together.

And summer brings choice enough to please
an avid blairite: plant on plant,
a whole spectrum. "I'm the bee's knees",
"No, me", "O, how I try but can't:
they're shoving".
        This is your tiptop 'riot
of colour', call in the fuzz to quiet.

There will always be green to cheer
things up: shields, clapped palms, umbrellas,
foil, trefoil, quatrefoil, spear –
for innocence, for the Levellers,
the wearing of …
                              and always grass
that Clare so worshipped for commonplace.

Best to look high meantime, with sight
perching on leaf and blossom-burst –
that spectrum spinning until all turn white,
even rowan's promised spurts
of blood, October's blood-rust.
                                                Jump
the gun no doubt, but the future's coming.

MARTHA'S CAPABLE KITCHEN

"... and it's such a capable kitchen – there's such good dark corners in it – I'd be
bound to hide anyone".

(Elizabeth Gaskell, *Cranford*)

In time, we know, Martha will get her man:
there seems to have been wide choice
and, to her predecessor, Fanny,
this has already proved a capable place.

In terms of maids of all work, wider than mating
patterns too, matters
are simple enough. And yet, and yet ...
Time is on time for us, but the *place* loiters.

On time for change, that is: the dark corners
Martha considers good ...
Change for us, that is, who yearn as
desperately ... Something that the world would ...

If where *we* are is capable, that is.
For Fanny coat-tails dis-
appeared between back-door and clock
and a weirdly-dimensional shadow suggested bulk.

Suppose other desires could grab their spouse
from risking a barked shin
in the dark. Why, every corner in the house,
all Cranford, the global want of Peace would grin

as day faded and shadows filled to the brim
of time and place, with reason
proportionate to Martha's eventual Jem
"six foot one in his stocking-feet, please ma'am".

FORMS OF LOWLIFE

The word (or weed) *mad* for instance.
Pick it, but mind the environment you find;
don't dig or fence it. Ants – in
general, *pismires* – dodge all species
of *mad*, turning the blind
eye of pretence that they're not here.

Also look out for *cuckoospit*
that lands on *mad* to play the frothing critic.
Rather be butterfly
or bee, searching to take but giving
too, the let-live scholars.
Pick *mad* – gently – as you go indoors.

Look up dialect word-lists – *nutcase*,
loony, peasant – slipping your eye down-page
to meadowsweet, to reedmace
and other familiar weeds beyond
but picking the nicknames, fondnames
got often of disdain or rage.

Better with birds (as he is) there's yet
edding, elting, brake, bent, tattlegrass, keck,
horse-bleb or *water-blab* –
for *paddock* and *bumbarrel* to light
on, birds favoured by *mad*.
And now that day has collapsed, let night

blur boundaries. Find reference
to *commons* where dialect grew, and *customs*
which Privilege had fenced
against. For topics, look up Raging
*Mad*ness; lowlife, Care
in Confinement, or Not; also John Clare

who after all is no more sweet
than when enraged. *Carfart, landfill, oilslick,*
spewfarm, treehack, spoilheap,
fatcat. Dirtying Privilege still
destroys. *Mad* is endangered.
And what species is not for the kill

called profit? *Pismire* and *cuckoospit*
evade and froth. Give *case* back to its *nut.*
Never be *sane* and despair.
Open the poems, read John Clare.
Old man, become a lad
down here, low down. Cherish *mad.*

RAILWAY DIVERSION

for Liz Shaw

Landscape whizzes, and headlines shout
Queen Feasts Mandela. That Red,
snorts a fellow passenger, stuffing his tory
face. It's what they leave unsaid,
he continues darkly.
                              Saunter down
that long first class from which She's bred –
Windsor from Hanover from Orange,
Stuart, Tudor, Plantagenet –
all those remembered monarchs dead
of pillows, pox, pokers up the arse,
kingdoms for horses, let's have His head.

Sooner or later beside the line
strange informations lodge like half-read
station nameplates, 'til we are side-tracked,
shunted into a gloomy shed
along with Stephen and Matilda.*

Now She, Matilda (or Maud), was wed
to Geoffrey son of Fulk (or Fuck)
the Fifth, a junction towards which had sped
Fulk the Fourth, the Third, the Second
(or Good – peacefully, in His bed).
A brake squeals. We've hit the buffers.
The first Fulk was Fuck the Red.

*From here on I follow John Harvey, *The Plantagenets* 1951

69

THE FRIGGER ANNEXE

1: BANNERS

for Andy Croft

We didn't make the banners of course.
Professionals did them. But they were ours
in a larger public sense than tradeforce,
region, family, narrow purpose.
Ragworks or things made out of leavings
wouldn't do for what we believed in.

Nor would a mate's invention do
for causes larger than a me and you.
And so we paid for portraits of founders,
workscenes, services members could count on.

You know the result, or saw the like
on a newsflash during the great coal strike.

Likeness (you see) had never been
our art, but a vision (you have to imagine).

Colour was ours, the swaggering bunting
effect, trumpets and drums up front,
and something the scale of a kingsize bedspread
flaring about us overhead.

You see few of them now. Defeat
has left them rolled in cupboards. And yet
sometimes we march. And when, at Greenham
or Treekeep, people arise, between them
a flaunt of blazons begins to appear
in patchwork, from rags – ours for sure.

2: TRENCH ART 1914–1918

for John Lucas

Chiefly, since it's the only waste
material here save flesh and bone,
most things we frig out of shell-cases –
like scratch your heart out on the brazing.
(At Base, though, bone-dry, on grass, sent back
with a blighty, I've seen a no-legs cut up a
patchwork out of the union jack).

Back in the Line, what's yours? Army
biscuit? Mud won't soggy that
but toughs it to iron, well carvable
when dry. You won't mind ration-starving.

Or cut off badges (cloth or metal)
from parts of who's new on the death-roll

(for peace-work, memories, out of this ditch
of no-grass). Plenty of oddsods. Over
at Wipers, Gurney is setting *Even such
is Time* for a song. Well, good on yer, Ivor!

Sgraffito mess-tins? Burnish the etch
with mud, buffs up a treat, class
finish. Always we've furnished ourselves
out of surplus – wastage, offcuts, dead'uns.
The Line stretches like Time. Mud
and its few friggers! But there's to be grass
at last, John Clare (signalman) said.

3: PIGEON CREES, ASHINGTON

i.m. Martin Taylor

Beyond the backs, among allotments
each cree stands easy. Soil was at worst
out here through tip-spillage, dirt
from the stack, the gritty rail-roaded pit.
How could a lad like all of it?

But the crees are brave in paint-and-paint-
again their particoloured flanks,
lath turrets, pigeonports – if gunless
and gaudy, tanks in a No Man's Land.

The pits long shut, still pigeon
flights fire off out of stuck-in-the-mud
air-castles, lop-limbed as religion.

                    *

He left for London, to the War Museum,
loved Owen and Gurney, edited *Lads* *
whose poems were metred by the gun-thud.

Hankering home where the rhymes began,
bigots were by: sad homophobic
fuckwits, artless, frigger-fanciers
cooing the sky for their pretties homing.

We never agreed about the crees:
pitwork and fancy; beauty and dross;
dole, pigeon; squaddie, dove.
And it's too late now to be argued and cross
barbed lines, as once, to speak of love.

*Martin Taylor, *Lads, Love Poetry of the Trenches*, 1989

4: SHEILA'S COLLECTION

for Sheila Gilbert

Above the sink they hang, aligned
on the face of rafters, easy for washers-
up to contemplate – her finds,
most of them spoons, the smaller kinds.

One fork, four pastry-cutters hang
there too, more intricate perforce
but the spoons don't seem to give a damn.

Carved out of horn, a tusk, bone,
various woods – one silver but foreign –
she's found none lately, told they have gone
to lackpast Americans come touring

through junkshops, fleamarkets, car-boot sales
in the Isle of Man, Lancashire, Wales.

Smaller spoons she reckons for mustard
or spice, larger for eggs or carting
a sweetener for scrape – in places where custom
flirted with handcraft, giggled at art.

Down here, though, where she cleans the veg
the spoons proclaim no use, only
their charms that hide a secret knowledge.

'Keen as mustard' no doubt. At 'spooning'?
(I carved it for you, sweet picaroon,
my pepper, my honey, my hen) – in delight
far beyond a muncher's appetite.

5: THE FRIGGING FOLK

i.m. Hamish Henderson

Cyrenaica: there he mourned
all swaddies, "death's proletariat"
he called them, voiceless believing burned-out
balladeers, bodyparts war-blown
frigging the desert.
                    And after that,
Blairgowrie: berrypickers' songs
tumbling about him "like sitting" he said
"under Niagara with a tin
cup". Lucky bugger. The longing
we'd all of us shared to be poets and read
or heard where Folk took poems in
like christchilds.
                    And the rest of us?
What of the rest who only picked at
the shards? *Gwalia Deserta?*
*Cara Wallia Derelicta?**

In the end to *Embro, Sandy Bell's*:
his court where the Folkworld came, wee drams,
long pints, old songs, old ways
to sing, the old auld languages
beside his new-seeming to ourselves.
Hark at him, just!
                    Well, christdammit,
we have "mair nor a roch wind blawin
through the great glen o' the warld the day".
Which being surely so, we mourn?

*Titles by the Welsh poets Idris Davies and David Jones. Their chief works derive
from South Wales coalmining valleys and First World War trenches respectively.

6: BUCHAREST FOLK MUSIC FINALS, 1950s

i.m. A.L. Lloyd

All the competitors, losers included,
resplendent in costume, instruments proud
as a People in decoration and colour,
stood in a row, grinning. *Grand
Finale, People's Republic's anthem:
Altogether now !* Strewth, what a hulla-
balloo! Who could hear any tune
in such a unison? First rage,
then misery, getting somehow off stage.

We *always* cut the *fluer* from the one
particular tree, said the shepherd: custom
demands it of us. Same with the *bucium*
(a sort of alphorn), said another, wheezy
from blowing. Can't they work out that a goatskin
depends on the size of the goat and determines
my *cimpoi*? protested the squeezer-geezer.

Much the same for players (and makers)
of *caval, nai, cobza, tambal.*
Do they understand music at all?
The bloody village is ours, for pete's sake.
Bollocks to 'Pitch must be National'!

And we who sat and watched the assembled
disperse, the grins grow false, and trembled,
pray that understanding remembers.

7: AMERICAN DECOY DUCKS

for John Davies

The way John Davies tells it (who carves
in wood as well as language), two
barber brothers Ward, one painting
what the other carved, working by halves
that is, were champions of all the U
SA contestants in decoy-making.

Had to be like enough to fool
the actual birds of course, persuadable
enough for buyers. And beautiful?

Well, what would you define as beauty?
Aptness of form to material?
Purpose – though surely potting at ducks
is not enough? A sense of duty
to present some wonderful truth to the whole
wide world of America? "Aw, shucks"

(though it's not often you hear himself –
decoy from wood from tree from nut
from the words of men inside that nutshell)

"You had to live into it", said Steve
the carver, birdwatch to knife to brush
(that's Lem), the whole of your life cuddling
from barbershop hubbub a duck-like hush,
so "We didn't pattern from nobody.
All we borrowed from was memory".

8: A HOLE-MAKER CARVED IN BONE

to Myfanwy

who sent it to me, and whose father Edward Thomas, then a corporal in World
War I, famously wrote of "her own world … Wanting a thousand little things /
That time without contentment brings"

Smaller even than a sardine-can
opener, but also exquisite
beyond any function woman or man
could consider in desperate want of it:

A frigger? you ask, in sending me
so great a gift. Such a little thing –
one of the thousand, is it, that he
wrote 'time without contentment brings'?

whose time contained such discontented
want of change as yours or mine
that yet contains this competence
to make of Bone some other kind
than bone.

      'What!' protested the gypsy,
'Buy a broom in May!
and sweep one of the family away?'
So, to pick something, you purchased this
little thing.

      Made from a stewbone?
Or litter tidyings? Hole-maker? Anyway
frigger, for sure: pointed, new-grown,
knife-whittled, thumb-polished, merry-thought, penny-pinched.

Made of rejection, still it brings
contentment into this world containing
it – exemplary of change,
pricking me on to the immense things.

77

9: CONVICT TOKENS 1815–1830

for John Lucas

By now you've nothing but a hulk's deck
awaiting Transportation: thieves,
forgers, luddites – with only love
to leave as payment for penn'orths of debt.

Somehow, between hulk and shore
grows up a trade in other poor
and 'soft' mintings – the 'cartwheel' pennies
of George the Third common as any.
Grind off his head, unrule Britannia
'til surfaces are flattened to bland and a-

gog for design. Etch it, or follow
some cleverer fellow's pencilled-in line
dotting it bang on a nail's head.
(Scriveners here aboard for fraud? –

such elegant pencillings remain).
Read now, on tokens hidden in shame
for years, 'Your most affectionate son'
or 'Love me true', with illustration
forget-me-nots, parents, or a Man o' War –
your Transport perhaps, for Peace meant Fear.

From the world's end where you are bound
for a sentence living upside down,
here's the last scratch of a luddite's wreck,
a thief's take, old lover's work.

10: PEOPLE'S REPUBLIC OF COLOUR, RUMANIA 1954

for Alun Hughes

Some colours came by pounding, others
by boiling a special root, and sometimes
berryjuice, petals, metals, rusts.
No stain ever went unobserved.

Separate groups did the collecting –
troops of children, matriarchs, bovverboys,
old men, newlyweds – each with a habit
of colour. The village in-gathered a palette
to suit what the mothers wove, perfecting
texture, colour, equipoise.

Then the ministers and angels, the highs
and mighties, decreed: Not enough
of this wonderful village-by-village stuff!
We'll have to … How about aniline dyes!

They photo-matched the colours, put
in phones, constructed by-passes, sent
off truck upon truck to the furthest out.
There was – of course – no evil intent.
This was government, and the people's cause,
virtue – of course of course of course.

Back at the village folk started, stopped.
Collectors had now no need to begin,
their presence confused the weavers, dropped
customs cracked. The sky fell in.

11: WHIMBRELS AND WOODCOCK, SPOTTED AT GLYN-Y-WEDDW

for John Davies

The birds have decoyed me at last. I'm shot,
though it wasn't a telescopic sight
nor photo-accuracy that got me –

invention, inaccuracies, rather:
the truth – discovering this time feather
would not resemble but *be* feather.

Working deeply through the grains of word
as poems do, something was odd
now you had turned your hand to wood.

Precise in form as ever, splicing
grain into grain; but then that painted
stippled plumage – a sort of icing

on a sort of cake. This time, though? No.
These three, whimbrels and woodcock, downfold
wings on backs as all birds do,

with chips and lozenges from other
woods marquetried so as to *be*,
and not gloss over, woodness or feather:

a plumage so totally unreal
it is to look Nature fresh in the eye
as hope, or a child's astonishment will.

As friggers pick up sweepings from the floor
in a maker's joy. As poems too
should you dust the words, to write more.

12: PERHAPS JOHN WESLEY

a note to myself at the end

Little contrivance, only wit
is required sometimes. As good as to say
the thing exists in Nature. You pick
it out and prink it – humbled, okay?

Here. This bovine vertebra.
Stood with its hollow downwards, the 'head'
(that round ball-joint) upwards, four
'wings' flap like a duvet on a bed
in turmoil or hands alas-ing in prayer.

You've picked it. Now the wit. Paint
all black except for a face on the 'head',
and parson's bands. Dealers have said
it's a flap-gowned preaching bullocking saint
from distant eighteenth-century Vestment
Wars: even, for laughs, John Wesley.*

The given, like this contrivable bone,
or Rumania fifty years ago,
or Hamish's hand-them-on-to-me songs –
the thing in Nature – are all also
Human Nature against the Alone.

But alone, if cause and community fail,
if Nature's picked bare, then pick your brains
to pieces – to reassemble
as new Nature or Poem. Forget humble.

*Methodism's Epworth Archive contains dozens of these vertebra pieces, all labelled John Wesley but laughing at him, which makes the attribution – in such an archive – seem odd.

The Frigger Makers (1994) contained eighteen poems, each about different kinds of workingclass artefact. The term 'frigger' was taken from the glass industry and applied generally, often adapted as verb or adjective. I daresay 'friggily' will appear in time, for I continue to write these 24-line pieces and probably always will. *The Frigger Annexe* contains twelve of them which peer in and out of the subject as often as poke about inside. The sequence begins with one rescued and reprinted from unhappy isolation in *Living Here* (1996).